bichon fri

understanding and caring for your breed

Written by
Elizabeth James

bichon frisé

understanding and
caring for your breed

Written by
Elizabeth James

Pet Book Publishing Company

Bishton Farm, Bishton Lane, Chepstow, NP16 7LG, United Kingdom.
881 Harmony Road, Unit A, Eatonton, GA31024 United States of America.

Printed and bound in China through Printworks International.

The 'he' pronoun is used throughout this book instead of the rather
impersonal 'it', however no gender bias is intended.

ISBN: 978-1-906305-74-1
ISBN: 1-906305-74-9

Acknowledgements

The publishers would like to thank the following for
help with photography: Chris Wyatt (Bobander);
Emma Roche (Rassau); Phil Shepherd (Calpastor).

Contents

Introducing the Bichon Frisé

Small, adaptable, full of character, and spectacular to look at, the Bichon Frisé is the perfect dog for 21st-Century living. Town or country, apartment or mansion, the Bichon will be happy to fit in, as long as he can be your constant companion.

Throughout his history, the Bichon has been a people dog, and he excels in this role. He is loving and affectionate, with a gentle side to he nature. But do not be misled into thinking that the Bichon is nothing but a pampered lapdog. He is a big dog in a small body; those dark, mischievous eyes, peeping through his stunning white coat, tell you all you need to know...

Physical characteristics

The Bichon is a small but sturdy dog, which sets him aside from the more delicate breeds of similar size. He is well balanced and compact, and the plumed tail, carried jauntily over his back, gives a further clue to his friendly, outgoing temperament.

His head is in proportion to his body, although when a Bichon is presented in the show ring, the round shape of the head, with its abundant coat, is the outstanding feature.

The Bichon has a beautiful white coat which falls in silky corkscrew curls. The contrast of the white coat with his dark eyes and black nose is striking. The workload of keeping a Bichon in full coat is immense, so many owners opt for a smart pet trim.

It is interesting to note that Bichon do not have the doggy odor you associate with many breeds. This is because they do not produce the same oils in their coat, and, as the Bichon tends to be bathed frequently, the oils they do produce are washed out.

Allergy sufferers

The great advantage of the Bichon coat is that it does not shed in the same way as most breeds, and is therefore is less likely to be a problem to allergy sufferers. However, you should not take this for granted, as dog saliva or dander can be an issue. The only way to check this out is to spend some time with the breed before making a decision. Responsible breeders will be happy to accommodate this, as their priority is to ensure that the puppies they produce go to suitable, forever homes.

Mad five minutes

A Bichon characteristic is a sudden explosion of energy and activity, which is best described as a 'mad five minutes'. A Bichon may be resting peacefully, get up and stretch – and then take off! A few circuits, at top speed, usually does the trick, and then a Bichon is happy to resume life at its normal pace...

Trainability

This is as breed with both brains and beauty, and you will be amazed at how quick your Bichon learns. The drawback is that he will be just as speedy at learning bad habits as good, so you will need to be on your guard.

The Bichon thrives on the opportunity to use his brain and will enjoy any type of training, as long as you make it fun. This is an exuberant and lively dog, quickly bored by anything he perceives as dull or repetitious.

You should also be aware that a Bichon can become too attached to his human family, so much so that he will pine if he is left on his own for any length of time. Although a Bichon should never be excluded from his family long periods, he needs to be able to cope with short separations. It is therefore important that you accustom your puppy to short spells of time when he is home alone, so that he understands that you go away – but you always come back!

On guard!

The Bichon is alert to everything that is going on, and he will give a warning bark (or barks) at the approach of strangers. He has a deep bark for a little dog, and visitors are often surprised when they are greeted by a diminutive breed. At this stage, the Bichon's role as guard dog tends to fall apart, as his way of assessing a stranger is to smother them in kisses...

Life expectancy

The Bichon is a breed without exaggeration, and most live a long, happy and health life. The average life expectancy is 12-13 years, although a fair number reach their mid-teens.

Tracing back in time

The Bichon Frisé has an ancient history, although its arrival on the show scene is relatively recent. There are references to small, white dogs living around the Mediterranean dating back more than two centuries BC.

The Bichon Frisé descends from the Barbet or Water Spaniel; it became known as the 'barbiche', meaning 'beard', which was then shortened to Bichon.

There are four breeds in the Bichon family:

- Bichon Maltais (Maltese)

- Bichon Bolognais (Bolognese)

- Bichon Havanais (Havanese)

- Bichon Tenerife (later known as the Bichon Frisé).

The Mediterranean was an important trading area, and Bichon dogs were frequently used for barter.

This meant they were taken all over the world, and the four Bichon types developed independently.

Among the exotic destinations was Tenerife, the largest of the Canary Islands off the west coast of Africa. The Bichon we are interested in soon became popular among the locals and was given the name Bichon Tenerife – a name he was to keep for several centuries.

Royal favorites

In the 1400s, Italian sailors introduced the Bichon Tenerife to Europe. The little, white dog was adopted as a royal favorite in the Italian court and flourished throughout the Renaissance period.

When France invaded Italy in the 16th century, Bichon were among the spoils of war, and they soon found a place in the royal court of France and in the homes of the French nobility.

Henry III (1574-1589) was so besotted by his dogs that he refused to be parted from them. He conducted the business of the nation with his favorite Bichon in a basket, tied around his neck with brightly-colored ribbons!

Street dogs

The Bichon Tenerife enjoyed royal favor until the latter part of the 19th century, but then suffered a dramatic fall from grace. The breed was no longer sought after as a status symbol, but was left to roam the streets, living among commoners and surviving on scraps.

However, the clever little Bichon proved resourceful. Travelers discovered that these street urchins were remarkably bright and could be taught to perform tricks. Soon they were traveling in performing troupes, delighting circus crowds and visitors to village fairs throughout Europe.

The Havanese is one of the four breeds that make up the Bichon family.

Developing
the breed

The Bichon Tenerife proved successful as a performing dog, but the future of the breed looked uncertain as bloodlines became increasingly diluted. Fortunately, the Bichon's charm and good looks found new recognition.

The Bichon Tenerife survived as best as he could during the early part of the 20th century, and during the First World War (1914-1918). But then his fortunes took a turn for the better. Soldiers returning from the war brought home the little white dogs they found in various European countries, and they came to the attention of French and Belgian dog enthusiasts.

Breed recognition

There was only limited stock available, but breeders got to work to increase numbers, thereby safeguarding the breed. In March 1933, Madame Boutovangniez, President of the French Toy Club, devised a Breed Standard in conjunction with the Friends of Belgian Breeders, and the Bichon's future looked assured.

There was great debate over naming the 'new' breed. The name Bichon Tenerife had been dropped in favour of Bichon a Poil Frisé, meaning 'Bichon of the curly hair', but no agreement could be reached on finding an official name. Finally, the head of the Breed Standards Committee for the European Kennel Club, Madame Nizet de Leemans, simply asked what then breed looked like. The answer was "a fluffy, little dog" – Bichon Frisé – and the name has stuck.

Two-way traffic

It was 1956 when the first Bichon arrived in the USA. Helene and Francis Picault of Dieppe, France emigrated to Milwaukee, Wisconsin, taking with them a mini pack of seven Bichon Frisé.

Starting with this very limited gene pool, the breed was slowly established in its new home as breeders took an interest in the showy white dogs that also made outstanding companions.

In 1964 the Bichon Frisé Club of America was founded, but there was a considerable delay before the breed received official recognition from the American Kennel Club. It was accepted for entry in the Miscellaneous Class in 1971 and two years later it received full recognition as a member of the Non-Sporting Group.

Despite its proximity to France, the UK was slow to catch on to the new breed. In 1973 American breeders, Mr and Mrs E Sorstein, emigrated to the UK, bringing with them their two Bichon, Rava's Regal Valor of Reenroy and Jenny-vive de Carlise. They produced a litter of five pups, which were to be the foundation of the breed in the UK.

Today, the Bichon Frisé has a worldwide following, and is in the top thirty most popular breeds in both the UK and the USA. This little, white dog has found recognition as a glamorous show dog and, most important of all, as a companion dog *par excellence*.

What should a Bichon look like?

The eye-catching Bichon Frisé draws admiring glances wherever he goes with his glorious white coat, his melting dark eyes, and, perhaps most of all, his gay, extrovert attitude to life. So what makes a Bichon so special?

The aim of breeders is to produce dogs that are sound, healthy, typical examples of their chosen breed, in terms of both looks and temperament To achieve this, they are guided by a Breed Standard, which is a written blueprint describing what the perfect specimen should look like.

Of course, there is no such thing as a 'perfect' dog, but breeders aspire to produce dogs that conform as closely as possible to the picture in words presented

by the Breed Standard. In the show ring, judges use the Breed Standard to assess the dogs that come before them, and it is the dog that, in their opinion, comes closest to the ideal, that will win top honors.

This has significance beyond the sport of showing, for it is the dogs that win in the ring that will be used for breeding. The winners of today are therefore responsible for passing on their genes to future generations and preserving the breed in its best form.

There are some differences in the wording of the Breed Standard depending on national kennel clubs; the American Standard is certainly more descriptive than the English version. In the USA, the Bichon is placed in the non-sporting group of breeds, whereas in the UK, it is classified as a toy breed.

General appearance

The Bichon Frisé is a smart, well-balanced dog, with a proud head carriage and a plumed tail carried over his back. The American Standard describes him as "a small, sturdy, white powder puff of a dog" which sums him up to perfection.

Temperament

The Bichon has an impeccable temperament – gay, lively and playful.

Head and skull

This is very much a 'head breed', meaning that this is a distinguishing feature of the breed, although it must always be in proportion to the body. It can be hard to make out construction when the hair is trimmed to create a perfect ball shape, but, in fact, the skull is only slightly rounded. The muzzle should be longer than the skull in a ratio of three parts muzzle to five parts skull.

If a line is drawn between the outside corners of the eyes to the nose, it should create a near perfect equilateral triangle. The nose is prominent and is always black in color.

Eyes

The Bichon has beautiful dark eyes, which are round in shape and set in the skull to look directly forward. They are accentuated by dark haloes (well pigmented skin) surrounding the eyes. The expression is inquisitive and alert.

Ears

Again, these are virtually indistinguishable when a Bichon is in show coat, but they hang close to the head and are covered in flowing hair. The ear leathers are not as long as in a Poodle, where they reach the tip of the nose; they should extend no further than half the length of the muzzle.

The ears are set on slightly higher than eye level, and when the dog is alert, they are carried forward.

Mouth

The Bichon has strong jaws for a small dog and the teeth meet in a scissor bite – i.e. the teeth on the upper jaw closely overlapping the teeth on the lower jaw. The lips are fine and should always be black.

Neck

The neck is long and arched, measuring one-third the length of the body. The head should be carried proudly, and the neck should flow smoothly into the shoulders.

Forequarters

The shoulders are the same length as the upper arm and should be held close to the body. The legs are straight; they should be medium rather than finely-boned which contributes to the Bichon's sturdy appearance. The pasterns (the area between the wrist and the toes) is short, sloping slightly from the vertical when viewed from the side.

Body

The chest is well developed and wide enough to allow free and unrestricted movement of the front legs. The loin (the dog's 'waist') is muscular. The length of body from the withers (the highest point of the shoulders) to the tail set is equal in height as the withers are from the ground.

Hindquarters

The thighs are broad and muscular. The stifle (the dog's knee) is medium boned and well angulated.

Feet

Neat, round and cat-like, the feet should have black pads and black nails.

Tail

The tail is set level with the back and curves gracefully, so the hair lies along the topline. Tightly curled or corkscrew tails are considered highly undesirable.

Movement

The cheerful, extrovert character of the Bichon is epitomised by the way he moves – free, precise and effortless. In trot, the forelegs and hindlegs extend equally, while maintaining a level topline. The head and neck remain reasonably erect, giving the Bichon his proud bearing. Watch out for the rear footpads, which you can see when a Bichon is moving away from you.

Coat

The American Breed Standard states that the texture of the coat is of "utmost importance". The undercoat is soft and dense, the outer coat is soft to the touch with corkscrew curls which should measure 3-4 inches (7-10 cm) in length. The overall impression is similar to plush or velvet, and when the coat is patted, it should spring back.

Color

There is only one color – white. The American Standard permits buff, cream or apricot shadings around the ears or on the body as long as they do not exceed 10 per cent of the total color. The KC Standard allows cream or apricot shading only up to the age of 18 months.

Size

Both males and females come within the same size stipulations. In the American show ring, preference is given to dogs between 9.5 and 11.5 inches (24-

29cm) while the UK Standard states that males and females should be 9-11 inches (23-28 cm).

Summing up

Although the majority of Bichons are pet dogs and will never be exhibited in the show ring, it is important that breeders strive for perfection and try to produce dogs that adhere as closely as possible to the Breed Standard. This ensures that the Bichon remains sound in mind and body, and retains the unique characteristics of this very special breed.

What do you want from your Bichon?

There are hundreds of dog breeds to choose from, so how can you be sure that the Bichon Frisé is the right breed for you? Before you take the plunge into Bichon ownership, weigh up the pros and cons so you can be confident that this is the breed that is best suited to your lifestyle.

Companion

Throughout his long history, the Bichon has been prized for his very special brand of companionship, and this remains true to this day. He was bred to be a people dog, and his *raison d'etre* is to be with his beloved family – snuggled up on a lap if possible.

If you want a Velcro dog to share your life, this is the

breed for you. But bear in mind that companionship comes at a price, and a Bichon will be thoroughly miserable if he is left for lengthy periods or excluded from family activities.

The Bichon is hugely adaptable and will suit owners of all ages, as long as he is given the care he needs. If you have very small children, it may be better to delay Bichon ownership until they are beyond the toddler age. A Bichon is sturdy for a little dog, but puppies are tiny and will not withstand rough handling, no matter how unintentional.

If you are getting on in years, a Bichon will be an affectionate companion, alternating periods of activity with times when he is happy to chill out with you. However, you will need to make sure that your Bichon does have the opportunity to get rid of his energy and has the opportunity to exercise, even if means employing a dog walker on a regular basis.

Show dog

Do you have ambitions to exhibit your Bichon in the show ring? This is a specialist sport, which often becomes highly addictive, but you do need the right dog to start with.

If you plan to show your Bichon, you need to track down a show quality puppy, and train him so he will perform in the show ring, and accept the detailed 'hands on' examination that he will be subjected to when he is being judged.

You will also have to become an expert groomer, or employ the services of a professional. The Bichon is very high maintenance in terms of show presentation, so you will need to be truly dedicated to this highly specialized art.

It is also important to bear in mind that not every puppy with show potential develops into a top-quality specimen, and so you must be prepared to love your Bichon and give him a home for life, even if he doesn't make the grade.

Sports dog

If you are interested having a dog to compete in one of the canine sports, you may be surprised to know that a Bichon fits the bill. He is a remarkably intelligent little dog, and has made his mark in competitive obedience and agility.

For more information, see Opportunities for Bichons on page 148.

What does your Bichon want from you?

A dog cannot speak for himself, so we need to view the world from a canine perspective to work out what a Bichon needs in order to live a happy, contented and fulfilling life.

Time and commitment

First of all, a Bichon needs a commitment that you will care for him for the duration of his life – guiding him through his puppyhood, enjoying his adulthood, and being there for him in his later years. If all potential owners were prepared to make this pledge, there would be scarcely any dogs in rescue.

The Bichon was bred to be a companion dog, and this is what he must be. If you cannot give your Bichon the time and commitment he deserves, you would be strongly advised to delay owning a dog until your circumstances change.

Practical matters

As already highlighted, the Bichon is one of the most adaptable of breeds. He requires exercise, but not as much as the larger breeds. However, he is very demanding in terms of coat care.

A Bichon needs daily grooming, regardless of whether you opt to keep him in a full coat or in a pet trim. A pet trim is easier to maintain, but you will need to budget for trips to the groomer every six weeks or so. Keeping a Bichon in show coat demands, time, patience and dedication – it is certainly not for the faint-hearted. However, many owners say they build up a close bond when they are grooming their dogs, and both dog and owner enjoy spending quality time together.

Mental stimulation

The Bichon is a clever dog and he needs mental stimulation to keep his brain occupied. A bored dog quickly becomes destructive, or he may develop other behavioral problems. He is not being 'naughty' as we understand it; he is simply finding an occupation to fill the empty hours.

As a Bichon owner, you must take responsibility for your dog's mental wellbeing. It does not matter what you do with him – training exercises, teaching tricks, trips out in the car, or going for new, interesting walks – all are equally appreciated, and will give your Bichon a purpose in life.

You also need to provide a sense of leadership so your Bichon knows you are the decision-maker in the family. If he is left to his own devices, this highly intelligent little dog will run rings round you.

Extra considerations

Now you have decided that a Bichon is the dog of your dreams, you can narrow your choice so you know exactly what you are looking for.

Male or female?

The debate of male versus female rages in the Bichon world. Some say males have beauty while females have brains. There are those that claim males are more loving and loyal, but other says it is the females who are most affectionate. The only certainty is that all dogs are individuals, so you can never second-guess temperament.

In terms of size, there is nothing to choose between them as both sexes are bred within the same size range. You may find a female slightly more difficult to care for as you will need to cope with her seasonal cycle, which will start at around seven to eight months of age, with seasons occurring twice yearly thereafter. During the three-week period of a season, you will need to keep your

bitch away from entire males (males that have not been neutered) to eliminate the risk of an unwanted pregnancy.

Many pet owners opt for neutering, which puts an end to the seasons, and also and has many attendant health benefits. The operation, known as spaying, is usually carried out at some point after the first season. The best plan is to seek advice from your vet.

An entire male may not cause many problems, although some do have a stronger tendency to mark, which could include the house. However, training will usually put a stop to this. An entire male will also be on the lookout for bitches in season, and this may lead to difficulties, depending on your circumstances.

Neutering (castrating) a male is a relatively simple operation, and there are associated health benefits. Again, you should seek advice from your vet.

More than one?

Bichons are sociable dogs and certainly enjoy each other's company. But you would be wise to guard against the temptation of getting two puppies of similar ages, or two from the same litter.

Unfortunately there are some unscrupulous breeders who encourage people to do this, but they are thinking purely in terms of profit, and not considering the welfare of the puppies.

Looking after one puppy is hard work, but taking on two pups at the same time is more than double the workload. House training is a nightmare as, often, you don't even know which puppy is making mistakes, and training is impossible unless you separate the two puppies and give them one-on-one attention.

The puppies will never be bored, as they have each other to play with. However, the likelihood is that they will form a close bond, and you will come a poor second.

If you do decide to add to your Bichon population, wait at least 18 months so your first dog is fully trained and settled before taking on a puppy.

An older dog

You may decide to miss out on the puppy phase and take on an older dog instead. Such a dog may be harder to track down, but sometimes a breeder may have a youngster that is not suitable for showing, but is perfect for a family pet. In some cases, a breeder may rehome a female when her breeding career is at an end so she will enjoy the benefits of getting more individual attention.

There are advantages to taking on an older dog, as you know exactly what you are getting. But the upheaval of changing homes can be quite upsetting, so you will need to have plenty of patience during the settling-in period.

Rehoming a rescued dog

We are fortunate that the number of Bichon that end up in rescue is relatively small, and this is often through no fault of the dog.

The reasons are various, ranging from illness or death of the original owner to family breakdown, changing jobs, or even the arrival of a new baby.

It is unlikely that you will find a Bichon in an all breed rescue centre, but the specialist breed clubs run rescue schemes, and this will be your best option if you decide to go down this route.

Try to find out as much as you can about a dog's history so you know exactly what you are taking on. You need to be realistic about what you are capable of achieving so you can be sure you can give the dog in question a permanent home.

Again, you need to give a rescued Bichon plenty of time and patience as he settles into his new home, but if all goes well, you will have the reward of knowing that you have given your dog a second chance.

Sourcing
a puppy

Your aim is to find a healthy puppy that is typical of the breed, and has been reared with the greatest possible care. Where to start?

A tried and trusted method of finding a puppy is to attend a dog show where your chosen breed is being exhibited. This will give you the opportunity to see lots of different Bichon Frisé, and although they may look then same at first glance, you will soon get your eye in and notice there are different 'types' on show. They are all purebred Bichon, but breeders produce dogs with a family likeness, and so you can see which type you prefer.

When judging has been completed, talk to the exhibitors and find out more about their dogs. They may not have puppies available, but most will be planning a litter, and you may decide to put your name on a waiting list.

Internet research

The internet is an excellent resource, but when it comes to finding a puppy, use it with care:

DO go to the website of your national Kennel Club.

Both the American Kennel Club (AKC) and the Kennel Club (KC) have excellent websites which will give you information about the Bichon as a breed, and what to look for when choosing a puppy. You will also find contact details for specialist breed clubs (see below).

Both sites have lists of puppies available, and you can look out for breeders of merit (AKC) and assured breeders (KC) which indicates that a code of conduct has been adhered to.

DO find details of specialist breed clubs.

On breed club websites you will find lots of useful information which will help you to care for your Bichon. There may be contact details of breeders in your area, or you may need to go through the club secretary. Some websites also have a list of breeders who have puppies available. The advantage of going through a breed club is that members will follow a code of ethics, and this will give you some guarantees regarding breeding stock and health checks.

DO not look at puppies for sale ads.

There are legitimate Bichon breeders with their own websites, and they may, occasionally, advertise a litter, although in most cases reputable breeders have waiting lists for their puppies. The danger comes from unscrupulous breeders who produce puppies purely for profit, with no thought for the health of the dogs they breed from and no care given to rearing the litter. Photos of puppies are hard to resist, but never make a decision based purely on an advertisement. You need to find out who the breeder is, and have the opportunity to visit their premises and inspect the litter before making a decision.

Questions, questions, questions

When you find a breeder with puppies available, you will have lots of questions to ask. These should include the following:

- Where have the puppies been reared? Hopefully, they will be in a home environment which gives them the best possible start in life.

- How many are in the litter?

- What is the split of males and females?

- How many have already been spoken for? The breeder will probably be keeping a puppy to show or for breeding, and there may be others on a waiting list.

- Can I see the mother with her puppies?

- What age are the puppies?

- When will they be ready to go to their new homes?

Facing page: Find out when the puppies will be ready to go to their new homes.

Bear in mind puppies need to be with their mother and siblings until they are eight weeks of age otherwise they miss out on vital learning and communication skills which will have a detrimental effect on them for the rest of their lives. Most breeders of small dogs prefer to keep the puppies a little longer – until they are 10 or 12 weeks old – when they are a little bigger and ready to face the world.

You should also be prepared to answer a number of searching questions so the breeder can check if you are suitable as a potential owner of one of their precious puppies.

You will be asked some or all of the following questions:

- What is your home set up?

- Do you have children/grandchildren?

- What are their ages?

- Is there somebody at home the majority of the time?

- What is your previous experience with dogs?

- Do you have plans to show your Bichon?

The breeder is not being intrusive; they need to understand the type of home you will be able to provide in order to make the right match. Do not be offended by this; the breeder is doing it for both the dog's benefit and also for yours.

Be very wary of a breeder who does not ask you questions. He or she may be more interested in making money out of the puppies rather than ensuring that they go to good homes. They may also have taken other short cuts which may prove disastrous, and very expensive, in terms of vet bills or plain heartache.

Health issues

In common with all purebred dogs, the Bichon suffers from a few hereditary problems. There are no health tests required for breeding stock at the moment, but you would be advised to talk to the breeder about the health status of their dogs and find out if there are any issues of concern. Although it is not mandatory, many breeders are now testing for hereditary cataracts (see page 186).

Puppy
watching

Bichon puppies have a charm all of their own; they look like tiny Polar bears, and when you see a litter you will want to take the whole lot home with you!

However, you must try to put your feelings to one side so that you can make an informed choice. You need to be 100 percent confident that the breeding stock is healthy, and the puppies have been reared with love and care, before making a commitment to buy.

Viewing a litter

It is a good idea to have a mental checklist of what to look out for when you visit a breeder. You want to see:

- A clean, hygienic environment.

- Puppies who are out-going and friendly, and eager to meet you.

- A sweet-natured mother who is ready to show off her babies.

- Puppies that are well covered, but not pot-bellied, which could be an indication of worms.

- Bright eyes, with no sign of soreness or discharge.

- Clean ears that smell fresh.

- No discharge from the nose.

- Clean rear ends – matting could indicate upset tummies.

- Lively pups that are keen to play.

It is important that you see the mother with her puppies as this will give you a good idea of the temperament they are likely to inherit. It is also helpful if you can meet other close relatives so you can see the type of Bichon the breeder produces.

In most cases, you will not be able to see the father (sire) as most breeders will travel some distance to find a stud dog that is not too close to their own bloodlines and complements their bitch. However, you should be able to see photos of him and be given the chance to examine his pedigree and show record.

Companion puppy

If you are looking for a Bichon as a companion, you should be guided by the breeder who will have spent hours and hours puppy watching, and will know each of the pups as individuals. It is tempting to choose a puppy yourself, but the breeder will take into account your family set up and lifestyle and will help you to pick the one most suitable.

Show puppy

If you are buying a puppy with the hope of showing him, make sure you make this clear to the breeder. A lot of planning goes into producing a litter, and although all the puppies will have been reared with equal care, there will be one or two that have show potential.

Ideally, recruit a breed expert to inspect the puppies with you, so you have the benefit of their objective evaluation. The breeder will also be there to help as they will want to ensure that only the best of their stock is exhibited in the show ring.

Look out for a puppy with the following attributes:

- A well-balanced body

- A broad skull

- Large, dark eyes, which should be surrounded by dark pigment (haloes)

- The lips, nose and pads should be black.

- The correct scissor bite (see page 30), although this cannot be guaranteed to remain correct once the adult teeth come in.

- A tail that is held over the back, but not touching it.

- An extrovert, outgoing temperament.

It is important to bear in mind that puppies go through many phases as they are developing. A promising puppy may well go through an ugly duckling phase, and all you can do is hope that he blossoms! However, if your Bichon fails to make the grade in the show ring, he will still be an outstanding companion who will be a much-loved member of your family.

An outgoing personality is essential in the show ring.

A Bichon-friendly home

It may seem an age before your Bichon puppy is ready to leave the breeder and move to his new home. But you can fill the time by getting your home ready, and buying the equipment you will need.

These preparations apply to a new puppy but, in reality, they are the means of creating an environment that is safe and secure for your Bichon throughout his life.

In the home

Nothing is safe when a Bichon is about – and that applies most particularly to puppies. The Bichon is lively, inquisitive and playful, and he will investigate everything he comes across. This could have disastrous consequences if an exploring puppy is given a free rein.

The best plan is to decide which rooms your Bichon will have access to, and make these areas puppy friendly.

Trailing electric cables are a major hazard and these will need to be secured out of reach. You will need to make sure all cupboards are secure, particularly in the kitchen, where you may store cleaning materials that could be toxic to dogs. Household plants can also be poisonous, so these will need to relocated, along with breakable ornaments.

Your puppy will be too small to negotiate stairs to begin with, so it may be easier to make upstairs off-limits right from the start. The best way of doing this is to use a baby gate, making sure your puppy cannot squeeze through, which could result in injury.

In the garden

You may think that secure fencing is only a necessity for large dogs, but small dogs are very talented at finding small gaps to squeeze through. You will therefore need to check all boundary fencing, just in case your Bichon finds an escape route. Gates leading from the garden should have secure fastenings.

If you are a keen gardener, you may want to protect your prized plants from unwanted attention. There are a number of flowers and shrubs that are toxic to dogs, so check this out on the Internet or by seeking advice from your local garden centre. You will also need to designate a toileting area. This will assist the house-training process, and it will also make cleaning up easier. For information on house training, see page 92.

House rules

Before your puppy comes home, hold a family conference to decide on the house rules. For example, is your Bichon going to be allowed to roam downstairs, or will you keep him in the kitchen unless you can supervise him elsewhere? When he is in the sitting room, is he allowed to come on your lap for a cuddle? These are personal choices, but if you have allowed your puppy to do something once, he will think that this is 'allowed', regardless of whether you change your mind. You and your family must make decisions – and stick with them – otherwise your puppy will be upset and confused, not understanding what you want of him.

Buying equipment

There are some essential items of equipment you will need for your Bichon. If you choose wisely, much of it will last for many years.

Indoor crate

Rearing a puppy is so much easier if you invest in an indoor crate. It provides a safe haven for your puppy at night, when you have to go out during the day, and at other times when you cannot supervise him. A puppy needs a base where he feels safe and secure, and where he can rest undisturbed. An indoor crate provides the perfect den, and many adults continue to use them throughout their lives.

You will also need to consider where you are going to locate the crate. The kitchen is usually the most suitable place as this is the hub of family life. Try to find a snug corner where the puppy can rest when he wants to, but where he can also see what is going on around him, and still be with the family.

Beds and bedding

The crate will need to be lined with bedding and the best type to buy is synthetic fleece. This is warm and cosy, and as moisture soaks through it, your puppy will not have a wet bed when he is tiny and is still unable to go through the night without relieving himself. This type of bedding is machine washable and easy to dry; buy two pieces, so you have one to use while the other is in the wash.

If you have purchased a crate, you may not feel the need to buy an extra bed, although many Bichons like to have a bed in the family room so they feel part of household activities. There is an amazing array of dog-beds to chose from – duvets, bean bags, cushions, baskets, igloos, and four posters – so you can take your pick! Before you make a major investment, wait until your puppy has gone through the chewing phase; you will be surprised at how much damage can be inflicted by small teeth.

Toys

The Bichon is one of the most playful of dogs, and he loves toys of all types. Any type of toy is suitable – squeaky toys, tug toys, rubber kongs, which can be filled with food, and soft toys.

Your guiding principle when choosing a toy must be whether it is suitably robust. You should also get into the habit of checking toys on a regular basis for signs of wear and tear. If your puppy swallows a chunk of rubber or plastic, it could cause an internal blockage. This could involve costly surgery to remove the offending item, or at worst, it could prove fatal.

Collar and leash

You may think that it is not worth buying a collar for the first few weeks, but the sooner your pup gets used to it, the better. All you need is a lightweight baby collar; you can buy something more exotic when your Bichon is fully grown.

A nylon leash is suitable for early leash training, but make sure the fastening is secure. Again, you can invest in a more expensive leash at a later date – there are lots of attractive collar and leash sets to choose from.

ID

Your Bichon needs to wear some form of ID when he is out in public places. This can be in the form of a disc, engraved with your contact details, attached to the collar. When your Bichon is full-grown, you can buy an embroidered collar with your contact details, which eliminates the danger of the disc becoming detached from the collar.

You may also wish to consider a permanent form of ID. Increasingly breeders are getting puppies' micro-chipped before they go to their new homes. A microchip is the size of a grain of rice. It is 'injected' under the skin, usually between the shoulder blades, with a special needle. It has some tiny barbs on it, which dig into the tissue around where it lies, so it does not migrate from that spot.

Each chip has its own unique identification number which can only be read by a special scanner. That ID number is then registered on a national database with your name and details, so that if ever your dog is lost, he can be taken to any vet or rescue centre where he is scanned and then you are contacted.

If your puppy has not been microchipped, you can ask your vet to do it, maybe when he goes along for his vaccinations.

Bowls

Your Bichon will need two bowls; one for food, and one for fresh drinking water, which should always be readily available. A stainless steel bowl is a good choice for a food bowl as it is tough and hygienic. Plastic bowls may be chewed, and there is a danger that bacteria can collect in the small cracks that may appear.

You can opt for a second stainless steel bowl for drinking water, or you may prefer a heavier ceramic bowl which will not be knocked over so easily.

Food

The breeder will let you know what your puppy is eating and should provide a full diet sheet to guide you through the first six months of your puppy's feeding regime – how much they are eating per meal, how many meals per day, when to increase the amounts given per meal and when to reduce the meals per day.

The breeder may provide you with some food when you go and collect your puppy, but it is worth making enquiries in advance about the availability of the brand that is recommended.

Grooming equipment

When your Bichon puppy first arrives, he does not need extensive coat care, but he needs to get used to being groomed. Initially you will need the following:

- A good-quality bristle brush

- A slicker brush

- A wide-toothed metal comb

- Guillotine nail clippers

- Toothbrush (a finger brush is easiest to use) and specially manufactured dog toothpaste

- Scissors to trim the coat

- Cotton-wool pads for cleaning the eyes and ears

- Mild dog shampoo.

Finding a vet

Before your puppy arrives home, you should register with a vet. Visit some the vets in your local area, and speak to other pet owners that you might know, to see who they recommend. It is so important to find a good vet, almost as much as finding a good doctor for yourself. You need to find someone you can build up a good rapport with and have complete faith in. Word of mouth is really the best recommendation.

- When you contact a veterinary practice, find out the following:

- Does the surgery run an appointment system?

- What are the arrangements for emergency, out of hours cover?

- Do any of the vets in the practice have experience treating Bichon?

- What facilities are available at the practice?

If you are satisfied with what your find, and the staff appear to be helpful and friendly, book an appointment do your puppy can have a health check a couple of days after you collect him.

Settling in

When you first arrive home with your puppy, be careful not to overwhelm him. You and your family are hugely excited, but the puppy is in a completely strange environment with new sounds, smells and sights, which is a daunting experience, even for the boldest of pups.

Some puppies are very confident, wanting to play straightaway and quickly making friends; others need a little longer. Keep a close check on your Bichon's body language and reactions so you can proceed at a pace he is comfortable with.

First, let him explore the garden. He will probably need to relieve himself after the journey home, so take him to the allocated toileting area and when he performs give him plenty of praise.

When you take your puppy indoors, let him investigate again. Show him his crate, and encourage him to go in by throwing in a treat.

Let him have a sniff, and allow him to go in and out as he wants to. Later on, when he is tired you can put him in the crate while you stay in the room. In this way he will learns to settle and will not think he is being abandoned.

It is a good idea to feed your puppy in his crate, at least to begin with, as this helps to build up a positive association. It will not be long before your Bichon sees his crate as his own special den and will go there as a matter of choice. Some owners place a blanket over the crate, covering the back and sides, so that it is even more cosy and den-like.

Meeting the family

Resist the temptation of inviting friends and neighbours to come and meet the new arrival; your puppy needs to focus on getting to know his new family for the first few days. Try not to swamp your Bichon with too much attention; give him a chance to explore and find his feet.

There will be plenty of time for cuddles later on!

If you have children in the family, you need to keep everything as calm as possible. Your puppy may not have met children before, and even if he has, he will still find them strange and unpredictable. A puppy can easily become alarmed by too much noise, or he may go to the opposite extreme and become over-excited, which can lead to mouthing and nipping.

The best plan is to get the children to sit on the floor and give them all a treat. Each child can then call the puppy, stroke him, and offer a treat. In this way the puppy is making the decisions rather than being forced into interactions he may find stressful.

If he tries to nip or mouth, make sure there is a toy at the ready, so his attention can be diverted to something he is allowed to bite. If you do this consistently, he will learn to inhibit his desire to mouth when he is interacting with people.

Right from the start, impose a rule that the children are not allowed to pick up or carry the puppy. They can cuddle him when they are sitting on the floor. This may sound a little severe, but a wriggly puppy can be dropped in an instant, sometimes with disastrous consequences

Involve all family members with the day-to-day care of your puppy; this will enable the bond to develop with the whole family as opposed to just one person. Encourage the children to train and reward the puppy, teaching him to follow their commands without question.

The animal family

Bichon enjoy the company of other dogs, but make sure you supervise early interactions so relations with the resident dog get off on a good footing.

Your adult dog may be allowed to meet the puppy at the breeder's, which is ideal as the older dog will not feel threatened if he is away from home. But if this is not possible, allow your dog to smell the puppy's bedding (the bedding supplied by the breeder is fine) before they actually meet so he familiarizes himself with the puppy's scent.

The garden is the best place for introducing the puppy, as the adult will regard it as neutral territory. He will probably take a great interest in the puppy and sniff him all over. Most puppies are naturally submissive in this situation, and your pup may lick the other dog's mouth or roll over on to his back. Try not to interfere, as this is the natural way that dogs get to know each other. You will only need to intervene if the older dog is too boisterous, and alarms the puppy.

It rarely takes long for an adult to accept a puppy,

particularly if you make a big fuss of the older dog so that he still feels special. However, do not take any risks and supervise all interactions for the first few weeks. If you do need to leave the dogs alone, always make sure your puppy is safe in his crate.

Meeting a cat should be supervised in a similar way, but do not allow your puppy to be rough, as the cat may retaliate by using his sharp claws. A Bichon puppy can be very excitable and may try running up and barking at the cat. Make sure you stop this straightaway before bad habits develop.

A puppy and a kitten may form a close bond if they are raised together.

Generally, the Bichon-feline relationship should not cause any serious problems. Indeed, many Bichon count the family cat among their best friends.

Feeding

The breeder will generally provide enough food for the first few days so the puppy does not have to cope with a change in diet – and possible digestive upset – along with all the stress of moving home.

Some puppies polish off their food from the first meal onwards, others are more concerned by their new surroundings and are too distracted to eat. Do not worry unduly if your puppy seems disinterested in his food for the first day or so. Give him 10 minutes to eat what he wants and then remove the leftovers and start afresh at the next meal.

Do not make the mistake of trying to tempt his appetite with tasty treats or you will end up with a faddy feeder. This is a mistake made by all too many Bichon owners, and a scenario can develop where the dog holds out, refusing to eat his food, in the hope that something better will be offered.

Obviously if you have any concerns about your puppy in the first few days, seek advice from your vet.

The first night

Your puppy will have spent the first weeks of his life either with his mother or curled up with his siblings. He is then taken from everything he knows as familiar, lavished with attention by his new family – and then comes bedtime when he is left all alone. It is little wonder that he feels abandoned.

The best plan is to establish a routine, and then stick to it so that your puppy knows what is expected of him. Take your puppy out into the garden to relieve himself, and then settle him in his crate. Some people leave a low light on for the puppy at night for the first week, others have tried a radio as company or a ticking clock. A covered hot-water bottle, filled with warm water, can also be a comfort. Like people, puppies are all individuals and what works for one does not necessarily work for another, so it is a matter of trial and error.

Be very positive when you leave your puppy on his own. Do not linger, or keep returning – this will make the situation more difficult. It is inevitable that he will protest to begin with, but if you stick to your routine, he will accept that he gets left at night – but you always return in the morning.

Rescued dogs

Settling an older, rescued dog in the home is very similar to a puppy in as much as you will need to make the same preparations regarding his homecoming. As with a puppy, an older dog will need you to be consistent, so start as you mean to go on.

There is often an initial honeymoon period when you bring a rescued dog home, where he will be on his best behavior for the first few weeks. It is after this that the true nature of the dog will show, so be prepared for subtle changes in his behavior. It may be advisable to register with a reputable training club, so you can seek advice on any training or behavioral issues at an early stage.

Above all, remember that a rescued dog ceases to be a rescued dog the moment he enters his forever home and should be treated like any other family dog.

Facing page: A rescued dog needs time to adjust to his new home.

House training

This is an aspect of training that most first-time puppy owners dread, but it should not be a problem as long as you are prepared to put in the time and effort.

Some breeders start the house training process by providing the litter with paper or training pads so they learn to keep their sleeping quarters clean. This is a step in the right direction, but most pet owners want their puppies to toilet outside.

As discussed earlier, you will have allocated a toileting area in your garden when preparing for your puppy's homecoming. You need to take your puppy to this area every time he needs to relieve himself so he builds up an association and knows why you have brought him out to the garden.

Establish a routine and make sure you take your puppy out at the following times:

- First thing in the morning

- After mealtimes

- On waking from a sleep

- Following a play session

- Last thing at night.

A puppy should be taken out to relieve himself every two hours as an absolute minimum. If you can manage an hourly trip out, so much the better. The more often your puppy gets it 'right', the quicker he will learn to be clean in the house. It helps if you use a verbal cue, such as "busy", when your pup is performing and, in time, this will trigger the desired response.

Do not be tempted to put your puppy out on the doorstep in the hope that he will toilet on his own. Most pups simply sit there, waiting to get back inside the house! No matter how bad the weather is, accompany your puppy and give him lots of praise when he performs correctly.

Do not rush back inside as soon as he has finished – your puppy might start to delay in the hope of prolonging his time outside with you. Praise him, have a quick game, and then you can both return indoors.

When accidents happen

No matter how vigilant you are, there are bound to be accidents. If you witness the accident, take your puppy outside immediately, and give him lots of praise if he finishes his business out there.

If you are not there when he has an accident, do not scold him when you discover what has happened. He will not remember what he has done and will not understand why you are cross with him. Simply clean it up and resolve to be more vigilant next time.

Make sure use a deodorizer, available in pet stores, when you clean up, otherwise your pup will be drawn to the smell and may be tempted to use the same spot again.

Choosing
a diet

There are so many different types of
dog food on sale – all claiming to be
the best – so how do you know what
is likely to suit your Bichon Frisé? He
may be small in size, but he is high
in energy and needs a well-balanced
diet that is suited to his individual
requirements.

**When choosing a diet, there are basically three
categories to choose from:**

Complete

This is probably the most popular diet, as it is
easy to feed and is specially formulated with all
the nutrients your dog needs. This means that you
should not add any supplements or you may upset
the nutritional balance.

Most complete diets come in different life stages: puppy, adult maintenance and senior, so this means that your Bichon is getting what he needs when he is growing, during adulthood, and as he becomes older. You can even get prescription diets for dogs with particular health issues.

There are many different brands to choose from, so it is advisable to seek advice from your puppy's breeder, who will have lengthy experience of feeding Bichon.

Canned/pouches

This type of food is usually fed with hard biscuit, and most Bichon find it very appetizing. However, the ingredients – and the nutritional value – do vary significantly between different brands, so you will need to check the label. This type of food often has a high moisture content, so you need to be sure your Bichon is getting all the nutrition he needs.

Homemade

There are some owners who like to prepare meals especially for their dogs – and it is probably much appreciated. The danger is that although the food is tasty, and your Bichon may appreciate the variety, you cannot be sure that it has the correct nutritional balance.

If this is a route you want to go down, you will need to find out the exact ratio of fats, carbohydrates, proteins, minerals and vitamins that are needed, which is quite an undertaking.

The BARF (Biologically Appropriate Raw Food) diet is another, more natural approach to feeding. Dogs are fed a diet mimicking what they would have eaten in the wild, consisting of raw meat, bone, muscle, fat, and vegetable matter.

Some owners worry that small breeds cannot cope with this diet, but there is evidence that they do well on it, particularly as many small dogs are prone to dental problems. The best plan is to seek advice from your vet.

Feeding regime

When your puppy arrives in his new home he will need four meals, evenly spaced throughout the day.

You may decide to keep to the diet recommended by your puppy's breeder, and if your pup is thriving there is no need to change. However, if your puppy is not doing well on the food, or you have problems with supply, you will need to make a change.

When switching diets, it is very important to do it on a gradual basis, changing over from one food to the next, a little at a time, and spreading the transition over a week to 10 days. This will avoid the risk of digestive upset.

When your puppy is around 12 weeks, you can cut out one of his meals; he may well have started to leave some of his food, indicating he is ready to do this. By six months, he can move on to two meals a day – a regime that will suit him for the rest of his life.

Bones and chews

Puppies love to chew, and many adults also enjoy gnawing on a bone. Bones should always be hard and uncooked; rib bones and poultry bones must be avoided as they can splinter and cause major problems. Dental chews, and some of the manufactured rawhide chews, are safe, but they should only be given under supervision.

Ideal weight

In order to help to keep your Bichon in good health it is necessary to monitor his weight. It is all too easy for the pounds to pile on, and this can result in serious health problems.

Facing page: Diet should be dictated by age and lifestyle.

The Bichon has perfected the art of looking at you with his melting dark eyes, and telling you he is 'starving', so you will need to harden your heart and think of his figure! If you are using treats for training, remember to take these into calculation and reduce the amount you feed at his next meal.

It can be hard to assess a Bichon's weight because of his curly coat, but a good guide is to look at him from above, and make sure you can see a definite 'waist'. You should be able to feel his ribs, but not see them.

In order to keep a close check on your Bichon's weight, get into the habit of visiting your veterinary surgery on a monthly basis so that you can weigh him. You can keep a record, so you can make adjustments to his feeding regime if necessary.

If you are concerned that your Bichon is putting on too much weight, consult your vet, who will help you to plan a suitable diet.

Facing page: Keep a close check on your Bichon's weight.

Caring for your Bichon

The Bichon Frisé is a high-maintenance breed when it comes to coat care, so you will need to schedule grooming sessions into your daily routine in order to keep your dog looking his best.

Puppy grooming

You would not have chosen a Bichon unless you were prepared to take care of his stunning white coat, and it is best if you start this from day one. If your puppy is accustomed to being groomed and handled from an early age, he will learn to accept the attention – and many actively enjoy it. This is essential for a dog that is going to spend a lot of time on the grooming table.

First, teach your puppy to stand on a table. It does not have to be a purpose-built grooming table – just one that is steady and is the right height for you to attend to your Bichon without getting backache. Place a rubber mat on the table so your puppy does

not slip and, to start with, let him sit or stand while you stroke him, and praise him for being calm. Reward him with a treat, and that will be sufficient for the first session.

The next day, you can introduce a pin bush, and groom him for a few minutes. The breeder will have started grooming sessions, so once your puppy feels confident with you, he should start to relax. The aim is to brush the coat in both directions, and then work through it with a comb to ensure there are no mats.

A Bichon's adult coat starts to come through from four months onwards, and you will probably find a slicker brush is more effective from this time onwards. Knots and mats are likely to appear as the coat changes, and you will find that a spray-on conditioner will help you to work through the coat more easily.

Pet trim

Many pet owners opt to keep their Bichon in a pet trim, This looks very smart and certainly cuts down on the huge workload associated with maintaining a full coat.

There are a number of styles to choose from:

- The coat on the body and legs is trimmed to half an inch (1.25 cm), leaving the hair on the tail, head and ears to grow long.

- A Poodle cut, where the hair is left longer on the legs, and the paws are given a very close clip.

- The coat is trimmed to half an inch all over, including the head, but the tail is left as a natural plume.

A pet trim is relatively easy to maintain.

Remember, even if you opt for a trim, your Bichon will still need regular grooming.

Bathing

Owning a white dog means bathing is a necessity, and so this is something else your puppy should be accustomed to from an early age. Always remember to groom before bathing, making sure the coat is free from mats and tangles.

You will need to use a shampoo specifically for dogs, and only use a conditioner now and again. It is essential that all traces of shampoo and conditioner are rinsed from the coat, as any residue could trigger skin irritation.

Bichon owners have their own preferences when it comes to frequency of bathing. The majority verdict is for a weekly bath, but show dogs will be need to be bathed before every show.

Show presentation

The Breed Standard for the Bichon is deceptive when it comes to show presentation. The UK Standard states that the breed may be untrimmed, or have the muzzle and feet "slightly tidied up". In fact, no dog would come into the show ring in his natural, untrimmed state, and the art of trimming is becoming ever more sophisticated.

The American Standard is a little more specific, stating that the Bichon should be trimmed "to reveal the natural outline of the body". It goes on to give more detailed instructions as to what is required, but his does not give a true picture of the sculptured outline that is now seen in the ring.

There is a huge amount of skill involved in trimming a Bichon coat, and most groomers work on the principle of little and often. They work at the coat a little every day, gradually enhancing its shape to achieve a graceful outline.

The head is the crowning glory of the Bichon, and the aim is to give a completely rounded appearance so the Bichon achieves the powder puff appearance that is characteristic of the breed.

Routine care

In addition to grooming, you will need to carry out some routine care.

Eyes

Check the eyes for signs of soreness or discharge. You can use a piece of cotton (cotton-wool) – a separate piece for each eye – and wipe away any debris. Some Bichon produce a mucous substance in their eyes and will, therefore, need daily care.

Tear staining is also prevalent, and there are a number of products that may help with this cosmetic problem. If applied on a regular basis, they will prevent the build-up of staining and keep the eyes clear and healthy.

Ears

The ears should be clean and free from odor. You can buy specially manufactured ear wipes, or you can use a piece of cotton (cotton-wool) to clean them if necessary. Do not probe into the ear canal or you risk doing more harm than good.

You will also need to pluck the hair that grows inside the ear. This is most easily done using finger and thumb. Start doing this from an early age, rewarding your puppy for his co-operation, so he learns to accept it without a fuss.

Teeth

Dental disease is becoming more prevalent among dogs, so teeth cleaning should be seen as an essential part of your care regime. This applies most particularly to small breeds, which tend to have more problems with their teeth. The build up of tartar on the teeth can result in tooth decay, gum infection and bad breath, and if it is allowed to accumulate, you may have no option but to get the teeth cleaned under anesthetic.

When your Bichon is still a puppy, accustom him to teeth cleaning so it becomes a matter of routine. Dog toothpaste comes in a variety of meaty flavours, which your Bichon will like, so you can start by

Wipe away the debris that accumulates around the eye.

Check the ears and clean if necessary.

Accustom your Bichon to teeth-cleaning from an early age.

Nails should be trimmed on a routine basis.

putting some toothpaste on your finger and gently rubbing his teeth. You can then progress to using a finger brush or a toothbrush, whichever you find most convenient.

Remember to reward your Bichon when he co-operates and then he will positively look forward to his teeth-cleaning sessions.

Nails

Nail trimming is a task dreaded by many owners – and many dogs – but, again, if you start early on, your Bichon will get used to the procedure.

Bichon have dark nails, which are harder to trim than white nails as you cannot see the quick (the vein that runs through the nail) and it will bleed if it is nicked. The best policy is to trim little and often so the nails don't grow too long, and you do not risk cutting too much and catching the quick.

If you are worried about trimming your Bichon's nails, go to your vet so you can see it done properly. If you are still concerned, you can always use the services of a professional groomer.

Exercise

The Bichon is small in size, but he is lively and energetic and will need regular, varied exercise.

Going for walks gives a dog the opportunity to use his nose and investigate new sights and smells, so even if he does not walk for miles, he will appreciate going to new places.

If, for any reason, your time is limited, it is useful if you can teach your Bichon to retrieve a toy. He will expend a lot of energy playing this game and he will also enjoy the mental stimulation. Bichon seem to love running together, and watching two fluffy, white dogs taking off at top speed, is an uplifting experience.

The older Bichon

We are fortunate the Bichon has a good life expectancy, and you will not notice any significant changes in your dog until he reaches double figures, or maybe even later.

The older Bichon will sleep more, and he may be reluctant to go for longer walks. He may show signs of stiffness when he gets up from his bed, but these generally ease when he starts moving. Some older Bichon may have impaired vision, and some may become a little deaf, but as long as their senses do not deteriorate dramatically, this is something older dogs learn to live with.

If you treat your older Bichon with kindness and consideration, he will enjoy his later years and suffer the minimum of discomfort. It is advisable to switch him over to a senior diet, which is more suited to his needs, and you may have to adjust the quantity, as he will not be burning up the calories as he did when he was younger and more energetic. Make sure his sleeping quarters are warm and free from drafts, and if he gets wet, make sure you dry him thoroughly.

Most important of all, be guided by your Bichon. He will have good days when he feels up to going for a walk, and other days when he would prefer to potter in the garden. If you have a younger dog at home, this may well stimulate your Bichon to take more of an interest in what is going on, but make sure he is not pestered as he needs to rest undisturbed when he is tired.

The older dog deserves special care and consideration.

Letting go

Inevitably there comes a time when your Bichon is not enjoying good quality of life, and you need to make the painful decision to let him go. We would all wish that our dogs died, painlessly, in their sleep but, unfortunately, this is rarely the case.

However, we can allow our dogs to die with dignity, and to suffer as a little as possible, and this should be our way of saying thank you for the wonderful companionship they have given us.

When you feel the time is drawing close, talk to your vet who will be able to make an objective assessment of your Bichon's condition and will help you to make the right decision.

This is the hardest thing you will ever have to do as a dog owner, and it is only natural to grieve for your beloved Bichon. But eventually, you will be able to look back on the happy memories of times spent together, and this will bring much comfort. You may, in time, feel that your life is not complete without a Bichon, and you will feel ready to welcome a new puppy into your home.

Social skills

To live in the modern world, without fears and anxieties, a Bichon needs to receive an education in social skills so that he learns to cope calmly and confidently in a wide variety of situations.

Early learning

The breeder will have started a program of socialization by getting the puppies used to all the sights and sounds of a busy household. You need to continue this when your pup arrives in his new home, making sure he is not worried by household equipment, such as the vacuum cleaner or the washing machine, and that he gets used to unexpected noises from the radio and television.

As already highlighted, it is important that you handle your puppy on a regular basis so he will accept grooming and other routine care, and will not be worried if he has to be examined by the vet.

To begin with, your puppy needs to get used to all the

members of his new family, but then you should give him the opportunity to meet people who come to the house. The Bichon is naturally friendly and outgoing, so this is rarely a problem. You will usually have the opposite problem... your Bichon being so enchanted by the visitor he won't leave them alone!

If you do not have children of your own, make sure your puppy has the chance to meet and play with other people's children, so he learns that humans come in small sizes, too.

The outside world

When your puppy has completed his vaccinations, he is ready to venture into the outside world. Most Bichon puppies take a lively interest in anything new and will relish the opportunity to broaden their horizons. However, there is a lot for a small puppy to take on board, so do not swamp him with too many new experiences when you first set out.

The best plan is to start in a quiet area with light traffic, and only progress to a busier place when your puppy is ready. There is so much to see and hear – people (maybe carrying bags or umbrellas), pushchairs, cycles, cars, lorries, machinery – so give your puppy a chance to take it all in.

If he does appear worried, do not fall into the trap of sympathizing with him, or worse still, picking him up. This will only teach your pup that he had a good reason to be worried and, with luck, you will 'rescue' him if he feels scared.

Instead, give a little space so he does not have to confront whatever he is frightened of, and distract him with a few treats. Then encourage him to walk past, using a calm, no-nonsense approach. Your pup will take the lead from you, and will realize there is nothing to fear.

Your pup also needs to continue his education in canine manners, started by his mother and by his littermates, as he needs to be able to greet all dogs calmly, giving the signals that say he is friendly and offers no threat. If you have a friend who has a dog of sound temperament, this is an ideal beginning. As your puppy gets older and more established, you can widen his circle of canine acquaintances.

Training classes

A training class will give your Bichon the opportunity to interact with other dogs, and he will also learn to focus on you in a different, distracting environment.

Before you go along with your puppy, it is worth attending a class as an observer to make sure you are happy with what goes on.

Find out if the instructors use reward-based training methods and if they have experience training small dog, and Bichons in particular. You should also check if the classes are divided into appropriate age categories.

If the training class is well run, it is certainly worth attending. Both you and your Bichon will learn useful training exercises; it will increase his social skills, and you will have the chance to talk to lots of like-minded dog enthusiasts.

Training guidelines

We are fortunate that the Bichon is a highly intelligent dog and is quick to learn. However, he is a dog with his own ideas and he needs to respect you and co-operate with you.

You will be keen to get started, but in your rush to get his training underway, do not neglect the fundamentals that could make the difference between success and failure.

When you start training, try to observe the following guidelines:

- Choose an area that is free from distractions so your puppy will focus on you. You can move on to a more challenging environment as your pup progresses.

- Do not train your puppy just after he has eaten or when you have returned from exercise. He will either be too full up, or too tired, to concentrate.

- Do not train if you are in a bad mood, or if you are short of time – these sessions always end in disaster!

- Make sure you have a reward your Bichon values – tasty treats, such as cheese or cooked liver, or an extra special toy.

- If you are using treats, make sure they are bite-size, otherwise you will lose momentum when your pup stops to chew on his treat.

- If you are using a toy as a reward, it should be used only when you are training so that it keeps its novelty value.

- Keep your verbal cues simple, and always use the same one for each exercise. For example, when you ask your puppy to go into the Down position, the cue is "Down", not "Lie Down", Get Down", or anything else... Remember, your Bichon does not speak English; he associates the sound of the word with the action.

- If your Bichon is finding an exercise difficult, break it down into small steps so it is easier to understand.

- Do not make your training sessions boring and repetitious; your Bichon will quickly lose interest.

- Do not train for too long, particularly with a young puppy, who has a very short attention span. Always end training sessions on a positive note.

- Above all, have fun so you and your Bichon both enjoy spending quality time together.

First lessons

A Bichon puppy will soak up new experiences like a sponge, so training should start from the time your pup arrives in his new home. It is so much easier to teach good habits rather than trying to correct your puppy when he has established an undesirable pattern of behavior.

Wearing a collar

You may, or may not, want your Bichon to wear a collar all the time; this may well depend on whether he is trimmed or in full coat. But when he goes out in public places he will need to be on a leash, and so he should be used to the feel of a collar around his neck. The best plan is to accustom your pup to wearing a soft collar for a few minutes at a time until he gets used to it.

Fit the collar so that you can get at least two fingers between the collar and his neck. Then have a game to distract his attention. This will work for a few

moments; then he will stop, put his back leg up behind his neck and scratch away at the peculiar itchy thing which feels so odd.

Bend down, rotate the collar, pat him on the head and distract him by playing with a toy or giving him a treat. Once he has worn the collar for a few minutes each day, he will soon ignore it and become used to it.

Remember, never leave the collar on the puppy unsupervised, especially when he is outside in the garden or when he is in his crate, as it is could get snagged, causing serious injury.

Walking on the leash

Once your puppy is used to the collar, take him outside into your secure garden where there are no distractions.

Attach the leash and, to begin with, allow him to wander with the leash trailing, making sure it does not become snagged up. Then pick up the leash and follow the pup where he wants to go; he needs to get used to the sensation of being attached to you.

The next stage is to get your Bichon to follow you, and for this you will need some tasty treats. You can show him a treat in your hand, and then encourage him to follow you. Walk a few paces, and if he is co-operating, stop and reward him. If he puts on the brakes, simply change direction and lure him with the treat.

Next, introduce some changes of direction so your puppy is walking confidently alongside you. At this stage, introduce a verbal cue "Heel" when your puppy is in the correct position. You can then graduate to walking your puppy outside the home – as long as he has completed his vaccination program – starting in quiet areas and building up to busier environments.

Do not expect too much of your puppy too soon when you are leash walking away from home. He will be distracted by all the new sights and sounds he encounters, so concentrating on leash training will be difficult for him. Give him a chance to look and see, and reward him frequently when he is walking forward confidently.

In the show ring, a Bichon wears a show leash, which is a very narrow slip-leash. A puppy will need extra training to show off his paces on leash, neither pulling ahead nor lagging behind.

Come when called

Teaching a reliable recall is invaluable for both you and your Bichon. You are secure in the knowledge that your dog will come back when he is called, and your Bichon benefits from being allowed off the leash and having the freedom to investigate all the exciting new scents he comes across.

We are fortunate that a Bichon likes to be with his people, and so he is unlikely to stray too far away. However, he may pick up an extra interesting scent or become distracted by meeting another dog. Obviously, you can allow him a little leeway, but you do want a dog who will come when he is called.

The breeder may have started this lesson, simply by calling the puppies to "Come" when it is dinnertime, or when they are moving from one place to another.

You can build on this when your puppy arrives in his new home, calling him to "Come" when he is in a confined space, such as the kitchen. This is a good place to build up a positive association with the verbal cue – particularly if you ask your puppy to "Come" to get his dinner!

The next stage is to transfer the lesson to the garden. Arm yourself with some treats, and wait until your puppy is distracted. Then call him, using a higher-pitched, excited tone of voice. At this stage, a puppy wants to be with you, so capitalize on this and keep practising the verbal cue, and rewarding your puppy with a treat and lots of praise when he comes to you.

Now you are ready to introduce distractions. Try calling him when someone else is in the garden, or wait a few minutes until he is investigating a really interesting scent. When he responds, make a really big fuss of him and give him some extra treats so he knows it is worth his while to come to you. If your puppy responds, immediately reward him with a treat.

If he is slow to come, run away a few steps and then call again, making yourself sound really exciting. Jump up and down, open your arms wide to welcome him; it doesn't matter how silly you look, he needs to see you as the most fun person in the world.

When you have a reliable recall in the garden, you can venture into the outside world. Do not be too ambitious to begin with; try a recall in a quiet place with the minimum of distractions and only progress to more challenging environments if your Bichon is responding well.

Do not make the mistake of only asking your Bichon to come at the end of a walk. What is the incentive in coming back to you if all you do is clip on his leash and head for home? Instead, call your dog at random times throughout the walk, giving him a treat and a stroke, and then letting him go free again. In this way, coming to you is always rewarding, and does not signal the end of his free run.

Stationary exercises

The Sit and Down are easy to teach, and mastering these exercises will be rewarding for both you and your Bichon.

Sit

The best method is to lure your Bichon into position, and for this you can use a treat, a toy, or his food bowl.

- Hold the reward (a treat or food bowl) above his head. As he looks up, he will lower his hindquarters and go into a sit.

- Practise this a few times and when your puppy understands what you are asking, introduce the verbal cue "Sit".

- When your Bichon understands the exercise, he will respond to the verbal cue alone, and you will not need to reward him every time he sits. However, it is a good idea to give him a treat on a

random basis when he co-operates to keep him guessing!

Down

This is an important lesson, and can be a lifesaver if an emergency arises and you need to bring your Bichon to an instant halt.

- You can start with your dog in a Sit or a Stand for this exercise. Stand or kneel in front of him and show him you have a treat in your hand. Hold the treat just in front of his nose and slowly lower it towards the ground, between his front legs.

- As your Bichon follows the treat he will go down on his front legs and, in a few moments, his hindquarters will follow. Close your hand over the treat so he doesn't cheat and get the treat before he is in the correct position. As soon as he is in the Down, give him the treat and lots of praise.

- Keep practicing, and when your Bichon understands what you want, introduce the verbal cue "Down".

Control exercises

These exercises are not the most exciting but they are useful in a variety of different situations. It also teaches your Bichon that you are someone to be respected, and if he co-operates, he is always rewarded for making the right decision.

Wait

This exercise teaches your Bichon to "Wait" in position until you give the next command; it differs from the Stay exercise, in which he must stay where you have left him for a more prolonged period. The most useful application of "Wait" is when you are getting your dog out of the car and you need him to stay in position until you clip on his lead.

- Start with your puppy on the lead to give you a greater chance of success. Ask him to "Sit" and stand in front him. Step back one pace, holding

your hand, palm flat, facing him. Wait a second and then come back to stand in front of him. You can then reward him and release him with a word, such as "OK".

- Practise this a few times, waiting a little longer before you reward him, and then introduce the verbal cue "Wait".

- You can reinforce the lesson by using it in different situations, such as asking your Bichon to "Wait" before you put his food bowl down.

Stay

You need to differentiate this exercise from the Wait by using a different hand signal and a different verbal cue.

- Start with your Bichon in the Down, as he is most likely to be secure in this position. Stand by his side and then step forwards, with your hand held back, palm facing the dog.

- Step back, release him, and then reward him. Practise until your Bichon understands the exercise and then introduce the verbal cue "Stay".

- Gradually increase the distance you can leave your puppy, and increase the challenge by walking around him – and even stepping over him – so that he learns he must "Stay" until you release him.

Leave

A response to this verbal cue means that your Bichon will learn to give up a toy on request, and it follows on that he will give up anything when he is asked, which is very useful if he has got hold of a forbidden object. You can also use it if you catch him red-handed raiding the bin, or digging up a prized plant in the garden.

Despite distractions your Bichon must learn to "Stay" in position.

Some Bichon can be a little possessive over their toys, and so it is important that your puppy learns that if he gives up something, he will get a reward, which may be even better than what he already has!

- The "Leave" command can be taught quite easily when you are first playing with your puppy. As you gently take a toy from his mouth, introduce the verbal cue, "Leave", and then praise him.

- If he is reluctant, swap the toy for another toy or a treat. This will usually do the trick.

- Do not try to pull the toy from his mouth if he refuses to give it up, as this will only make him keener to hang on to it. Let the toy go 'dead' in your hand, and then swap it for a new, exciting toy, so this becomes the better option.

- Remember to make a big fuss of your Bichon when he co-operates. If he is rewarded with verbal praise, plus a game with a toy or a tasty treat, he will learn that "Leave" is always a good option.

Facing page: Some Bichon can become possessive over their toys.

Opportunities
for Bichon

When the Bichon Frisé was fighting for his survival back in the 19th century, he found a new role as a performing dog in the circus. These days, Bichon live the life of pampered pets, but they still relish the opportunity to use their brains.

Agility

The Bichon is active and lively, and many have enjoyed considerable success in agility.

In this sport, the dog completes an obstacle course under the guidance of his owner. You need a good element of control, as the dog completes the course off the leash.

In competition, each dog completes the course individually and is assessed on both time and accuracy. The dog that completes the course in the fastest time, with the fewest faults, wins the class. The obstacles include an A-frame, a dog-walk, weaving poles, a seesaw, tunnels, and jumps.

Good Citizen Scheme

The Kennel Club Good Citizen Scheme was introduced to promote responsible dog ownership, and to teach dogs basic good manners. In the US there is one test; in the UK there are four award levels – Puppy Foundation, Bronze, Silver and Gold.

Exercises within the scheme include:

- Walking on leash
- Road walking
- Control at door/gate.
- Food manners
- Recall
- Stay
- Send to bed
- Emergency stop.

Competitive obedience

This is a sport where you are assessed as a partnership, completing a series of exercises including heelwork, recalls, retrieves, stays, sendaways and scent discrimination.

The Bichon is a quick thinker and likes to please, so he is more than capable of learning and performing the exercises. These are relatively simple to begin with, involving heelwork, a recall and stays in the lowest class, and, as you progress through, more exercises are added, and the aids you are allowed to give are reduced.

To achieve top honours in this discipline requires intensive training, as precision and accuracy are of paramount importance. However, you must guard against over training your Bichon, as he will quickly lose motivation.

Rally O

If you do not want to get involved in the rigors of Competitive Obedience, you may find Rally O is more to your liking.

This is loosely based on Obedience, and also has a few exercises borrowed from agility when you get to the highest levels. Handler and dog must complete a course, in the designated order, which has a variety of different exercises numbering from 12 to 20. The course is timed and the team must complete within the time limit that is set, but there are no bonus marks for speed.

The great advantage of Rally O is that it is very relaxed, and anyone can compete; indeed, it has proved very popular for handlers with disabilities as they are able to work their dogs to a high standard and compete on equal terms with other competitors.

Showing

If you plan to exhibit your Bichon in the show ring, you will need to be a dedicated groomer to ensure that your dogs look his very best when he is inspected by the judge.

You will also need to spend time training your Bichon to perform in the show ring. A dog that does not like being handled by the judge, or one that does not walk smartly on the leash, will never win top honours, even if he is a top-quality animal. To do well in the ring, a Bichon must have that quality that says: "look at me!", which proves that he is a real showman.

In order to prepare your Bichon for the busy show atmosphere, you need to work on his socialization, and then take him to ringcraft classes so you both learn what is required in the ring.

Showing at the top level is highly addictive, so watch out, once you start, you will never have a free date in your diary!

Heelwork to music

Also known as Canine Freestyle, this activity is becoming increasingly popular. Dog and handler perform a choreographed routine to music, allowing the dog to show off an array of tricks and moves, which delight the crowd. This is a brilliant discipline for the Bichon, giving him the perfect opportunity to show off his performing skills.

Health care

We are fortunate that the Bichon is a healthy dog and, with good routine care, a well-balanced diet, and sufficient exercise, most will experience few health problems.

However, it is your responsibility to put a program of preventative health care in place – and this should start from the moment your puppy, or older dog, arrives in his new home.

Vaccinations

Dogs are subject to a number of contagious diseases. In the old days, these were killers, and resulted in heartbreak for many owners. Vaccinations have now been developed, and the occurrence of the major infectious diseases is now very rare. However, this will only remain the case if all pet owners follow a strict policy of vaccinating their dogs.

There are vaccinations available for the following diseases:

Adenovirus (Canine Adenovirus): This affects the liver; affected dogs have a classic 'blue eye'.

Distemper: A viral disease that causes chest and

gastro-intestinal damage. The brain may also be affected, leading to fits and paralysis.

Parvovirus: Causes severe gastro enteritis, and most commonly affects puppies.

Leptospirosis: This bacterial disease is carried by rats and affects many mammals, including humans. It causes liver and kidney damage.

Rabies: A virus that affects the nervous system and is invariably fatal. The first signs are abnormal behavior when the infected dog may bite another animal or a person. Paralysis and death follow. Vaccination is compulsory in most countries. In the UK, dogs travelling overseas must be vaccinated.

Kennel Cough: There are several strains of Kennel Cough, but they all result in a harsh, dry, cough. This disease is rarely fatal; in fact, most dogs make a good recovery within a matter of weeks and show few signs of ill health while they are affected. However, kennel cough is highly infectious among dogs that live together so, for this reason, most boarding kennels will insist that your dog is protected by the vaccine, which is given as nose drops.

Lyme Disease: This is a bacterial disease transmitted by ticks (see page 166). The first signs are limping, but the heart, kidneys and nervous system can also be affected. The ticks that transmit the disease occur in specific regions, such as the north-east states of the USA, some of the southern states, California and the upper Mississippi region. Lyme disease is still rare in the UK so vaccinations are not routinely offered.

Vaccination program

In the USA, the American Animal Hospital Association advises vaccination for core diseases, which they list as: distemper, adenovirus, parvovirus and rabies. The requirement for vaccinating for non-core diseases – leptospirosis, lyme disease and kennel cough – should be assessed depending on a dog's individual risk and his likely exposure to the disease.

In the UK, vaccinations are routinely given for distemper, adenovirus, leptospirosis and parvovirus.

In most cases, a puppy will start his vaccinations at around eight weeks of age, with the second part given a fortnight later. However, this does vary depending on the individual policy of veterinary practices, and the incidence of disease in your area.

You should also talk to your vet about whether to give annual booster vaccinations. This depends on an individual dog's levels of immunity, and how long a particular vaccine remains effective.

Parasites

No matter how well you look after your Bichon, you will have to accept that parasites – internal and external – are ever present, and you need to take preventative action.

Internal parasites: As the name suggests, these parasites live inside your dog. Most will find a home in the digestive tract, but there is also a parasite that lives in the heart. If infestation is unchecked, a dog's health will be severely jeopardized, but routine preventative treatment is simple and effective.

External parasites: These parasites live on your dog's body – in his skin and fur, and sometimes in his ears.

Roundworm

This is found in the small intestine, and signs of infestation will be a poor coat, a pot belly, diarrhoea and lethargy. Pregnant mothers should be treated, but it is almost inevitable that parasites will be passed on to the puppies. For this reason, a breeder will start a worming program, which you will need to continue. Ask your vet for advice on treatment, which will need to continue throughout your dog's life.

Tapeworm

Infection occurs when fleas and lice are ingested; the adult worm takes up residence in the small intestine, releasing mobile segments (which contain eggs) that can be seen in a dog's feces as small rice-like grains. The only other obvious sign of infestation is irritation of the anus. Again, routine preventative treatment is required throughout your Bichon's life.

Heartworm

This parasite is transmitted by mosquitoes, and so will only occur where these insects thrive. A warm environment is needed for the parasite to develop, so it is more likely to be present in areas with a warm, humid climate. However, it is found in all parts of the USA, although its prevalence does vary. At present, heartworm is rarely seen in the UK.

Heartworm live in the right side of the heart. Larvae can grow up to 14in (35cm) in length. A dog with heartworm is at severe risk from heart failure, so preventative treatment, as advised by your vet, is essential. Dogs living in the USA should have regular blood tests to check for the presence of infection.

Lungworm

Lungworm, or *Angiostrongylus vasorum*, is a parasite that lives in the heart and major blood vessels supplying the lungs. It can cause many problems, such as breathing difficulties, blood-clotting, sickness and diarrhoea, seizures, and can even be fatal. The parasite is carried by slugs and snails, and the dog becomes infected when ingesting these, often accidentally when rummaging through undergrowth. Lungworm is not common, but it is on the increase and a responsible owner should be aware of it. Fortunately, it is easily preventable and even affected dogs usually make a full recovery if treated early enough. Your vet will be able to advise you on the risks in your area and what form of treatment may be required.

Fleas

A dog may carry dog fleas, cat fleas, and even human fleas. The flea stays on the dog only long enough to have a blood meal and to breed, but its presence will result in itching and scratching. If your dog has an allergy to fleas – which is usually a reaction to the flea's saliva – he will scratch himself until he is raw.

Spot-on treatment, which should be administered on a routine basis, is easy to use and highly effective on all types of fleas. You can also treat your dog with

a spray or with insecticidal shampoo. Bear in mind that the whole environment your dog lives in will need to be sprayed, and all other pets living in your home will also need to be treated.

How to detect fleas

You may suspect your dog has fleas, but how can you be sure? There are two methods to try.

Run a fine comb through your dog's coat, and see if you can detect the presence of fleas on the skin, or clinging to the comb. Alternatively, sit your dog on white paper and rub his back. This will dislodge feces from the fleas, which will be visible as small brown specks. To double check, shake the specks on to some damp cotton-wool. Flea feces consists of the dried blood taken from the host, so if the specks turn a lighter shade of red, you know your dog has fleas.

Ticks

These are blood-sucking parasites which are most frequently found in rural areas where sheep or deer are present. The main danger is their ability to pass lyme disease to both dogs and humans. Lyme disease is prevalent in some areas of the USA (see page 159), although it is still rare in the UK. The treatment you give your dog for fleas generally works for ticks, but you should discuss the best product to use with your vet.

How to remove a tick

If you spot a tick on your dog, do not try to pluck it off as you risk leaving the hard mouth parts embedded in his skin. The best way to remove a tick is to use a fine pair of tweezers or you can buy a tick remover. Grasp the tick head firmly and then pull the tick straight out from the skin. If you are using a tick remover, check the instructions, as some recommend a circular twist when pulling. When you have removed the tick, clean the area with mild soap and water.

Ear mites

These parasites live in the outer ear canal. The signs of infestation are a brown, waxy discharge, and your dog will continually shake his head and scratch his ear. If you suspect your Bichon has ear mites, a visit to the vet will be needed so that medicated ear drops can be prescribed.

Fur mites

These small, white parasites are visible to the naked eye and are often referred to as 'walking dandruff'. They cause a scurfy coat and mild itchiness.

However, they are zoonotic – transferable to humans – so prompt treatment with an insecticide prescribed by your vet is essential.

Harvest mites

These are picked up from the undergrowth, and can be seen as a bright orange patch on the webbing between the toes, although this can be found elsewhere on the body, such as on the ear flaps. Treatment is effective with the appropriate insecticide.

Skin mites

There are two types of parasite that burrow into a dog's skin. *Demodex canis* is transferred from a mother to her pups while they are feeding. Treatment is with a topical preparation, and sometimes antibiotics are needed.

The other skin mite is *Sarcoptes scabiei*, which causes intense itching and hair loss. It is highly contagious, so all dogs in a household will need to be treated, which involves repeated bathing with a medicated shampoo.

Common
ailments

As with all living animals, dogs can be affected by a variety of ailments. Most can be treated effectively after consulting with your vet, who will prescribe appropriate medication and will advise you on how to care for your dog's needs.

Here are some of the more common problems that could affect your Bichon, with advice on how to deal with them.

Anal glands

These are two small sacs on either side of the anus, which produce a dark-brown secretion that dogs use when they mark their territory. The anal glands should empty every time a dog defecates but if they become blocked or impacted, a dog will experience increasing discomfort. He may nibble at his rear end, or 'scoot' his bottom along the ground to relieve the irritation.

Treatment involves a trip to the vet, who will empty the glands manually. It is important to do this without delay or infection may occur.

Dental problems

The Bichon is less prone to dental problems than most of the small breeds, but good dental hygiene will do much to minimize gum infection and tooth decay. If tartar accumulates to the extent that you cannot remove it by brushing, the vet will need to intervene. In a situation such as this, an anesthetic will need to be administered so the tartar can be removed manually.

Diarrhoea

There are many reasons why a dog has diarrhoea, but most commonly it is the result of scavenging, a sudden change of diet, or an adverse reaction to a particular type of food.

If your dog is suffering from diarrhoea, the first step is to withdraw food for a day. It is important that he does not dehydrate, so make sure that fresh drinking water is available. However, drinking too much can increase the diarrhoea, which may be accompanied with vomiting, so limit how much he drinks at any one time.

After allowing the stomach to rest, feed a bland diet, such as white fish or chicken with boiled rice for a few days. In most cases, your dog's motions will return to normal and you can resume normal feeding, although this should be done gradually.

However, if this fails to work and the diarrhoea persists for more than a few days, you should consult you vet. Your dog may have an infection which needs to be treated with antibiotics, or the diarrhoea may indicate some other problem which needs expert diagnosis.

Ear infections

The Bichon has drop ears, and when a dog has a full show coat, they are virtually obscured by hair, so air will not circulate easily. This means that a Bichon is prone to ear infections.

A healthy ear is clean with no sign of redness or inflammation, and no evidence of a waxy brown discharge or a foul odor. If you see your dog scratching his ear, shaking his head, or holding one ear at an odd angle, you will need to consult your vet.

The most likely causes are ear mites, an infection, or a foreign body, such as a grass seed, trapped in the ear.

Depending on the cause, treatment is with medicated ear drops, possibly containing antibiotics. If a foreign body is suspected, the vet will need to carry our further investigations.

See Allergies, page 184.

Eye problems

The Bichon has large, round eyes; they are set in the skull and should not bulge. This is important, as breeds with prominent eyes, such as the Pekingese, are vulnerable to injury.

If your Bichon's eyes look red and sore, he may be suffering from conjunctivitis. This may, or may not be accompanied with a watery or a crusty discharge. Conjunctivitis can be caused by a bacterial or viral infection, it could be the result of an injury, or it could be an adverse reaction to pollen.

You will need to consult your vet for a correct diagnosis, but in the case of an infection, treatment with medicated eye drops is effective.

Conjunctivitis may also be the first sign of more serious inherited eye problems (see page 186).

In some instances, a dog may suffer from dry, itchy eye, which your dog may further injure through scratching. This condition, known as *keratoconjunctivitis sicca*, may be inherited.

Foreign bodies

In the home, puppies – and some older dogs – cannot resist chewing anything that looks interesting. The toys you choose for your dog should be suitably robust to withstand damage, but children's toys can be irresistible. Some dogs will chew – and swallow – anything, from socks, tights, and any other items from the laundry basket to golf balls and stones from the garden. Obviously, these items are indigestible and could cause an obstruction in your dog's intestine, which is potentially lethal.

The signs to look for are vomiting, and a tucked up posture. The dog will often be restless and will look as though he is in pain. In this situation, you must get your dog to the vet without delay as surgery will be needed to remove the obstruction.

Heatstroke

The Bichon's head structure is without exaggeration, which means that he has a straightforward respiratory system, and does not suffer breathing problems experienced by flat-nosed breeds, such as the Pug or the French Bulldog.

However, all dogs can overheat on hot days, and this can have disastrous consequences. If the weather is warm make sure your Bichon always has access to shady areas, and wait for a cooler part of the day before going for a walk. Be extra careful if you leave your Bichon in the car, as the temperature can rise dramatically - even on a cloudy day. Heatstroke can happen very rapidly, and unless you are able lower your dog's temperature, it can be fatal.

If your Bichon appears to be suffering from heatstroke, lie him flat and work at lowering his temperature by spraying him with cool water and covering him with wet towels. As soon as he has made some recovery, take him to the vet where cold intravenous fluids can be administered.

Lameness/limping

There are a wide variety of reasons why a dog can go lame – from a simple muscle strain, to a fracture, ligament damage, or more complex problems with the joints. If you are concerned about your dog, do not delay in seeking help.

As your Bichon becomes more elderly, he may suffer from arthritis, which you will see as general stiffness, particularly when he gets up after resting. It will help if you ensure his bed is in a warm, draft-free location, and if your Bichon gets wet after exercise, you must dry him thoroughly.

If your Bichon seems to be in pain, consult your vet who will be able to help with pain relief medication.

For more information on inherited disorders, see page 182.

Skin problems

If your dog is scratching or nibbling at his skin, first check he is free from fleas (see page 166). There are other external parasites which cause itching and hair loss, but you will need a vet to help you find the culprit.

As the Bichon is a white dog he tends to have more sensitive skin. In many cases, these are minor irritations, but in the case of an allergic reaction, it can cause major problems. It can be quite an undertaking to find the cause of the allergy, and you will need to follow your vet's advice, which often requires eliminating specific ingredients from the diet, as well as looking at environmental factors. *See Allergies, page 184.*

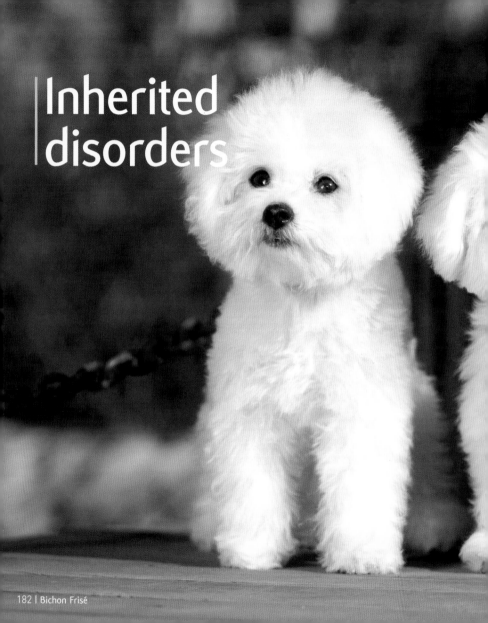

Inherited
disorders

Like all pedigree dogs, the Bichon Frisé does have a few breed-related disorders. If diagnosed with any of the diseases listed below, it is important to remember that they can affect offspring, so breeding from affected dogs should be discouraged.

There are now recognised screening tests to enable breeders to check for affected individuals and hence reduce the prevalence of these diseases within the breed.

DNA testing is also becoming more widely available, and as research into the different genetic diseases progresses, more DNA tests are being developed.

Allergies

Allergies are considered to be the number one health problem in Bichons, and these generally take the form of skin disorders. Skin sensitivity may vary in severity from minor, seasonal itching to full-blown skin disorders, which can have a major effect on a dog's comfort and wellbeing.

Allergies are the result of a hypersensitive response of the immune system, which may be triggered by:

- Flea bites (flea allergy dermatitis).

- Food (food allergies).

- Inhaled allergens, such as house and dust mites, grasses, moulds, tree and weed pollens (canine atopy).

- Irritants – materials such as rubber or plastic that have direct contact with the skin (contact allergies).

- Allergic dogs will itch and scratch, sometimes mutilating the skin, and will chew on their paws. They may also have recurrent ear infections.

The major problem is pinpointing what triggers the allergic reaction, which can only be done through a process of elimination.

Dogs suffering from allergies should be excluded from breeding programs.

Canine urolithiasis

This is a condition caused by stones or crystals in the urinary tract. In small breeds, such as Bichon, these can cause a blockage in the urethra (the tube from the bladder to the exterior). The likelihood of a blockage is more common in males as the urethra is longer and narrower.

If you see your Bichon urinating frequently, straining, or passing urine with blood, you should seek veterinary help without delay. Affected dogs should not be bred from.

Hereditary cataracts

These may affect one or both eyes. The clouding of the lens may be complete or partial, which will determine how much vision remains. Onset can be as early as six months or as late as seven years of age. Surgery to remove the cataract(s) can be effective, but there is a danger of complications.

The Canine Eye Registration Foundation (CERF), in the US, recommends annual eye testing, and affected dogs should not be bred from.

Legge perthes disease

This is a condition where the ball of the thigh bones dies before the skeleton matures, resulting in pain and lameness. It is generally seen in puppies aged four to six months. Early diagnosis, rest and pain relief may help, but surgery is often recommended.

Patellar luxation

This is a condition where the kneecap (patella) slips out of place or dislocates. The kneecap moves in a groove at the lower end of the femur (thigh bone). Some dogs – mostly small breeds – are born with a groove that is not deep enough to retain the kneecap, so that it pops out of place.

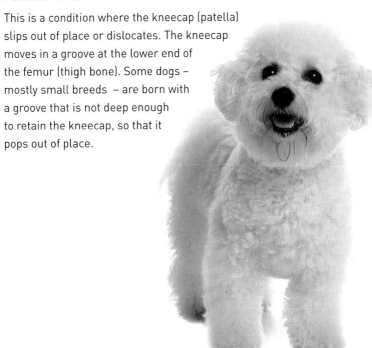

The characteristic sign is when a Bichon hops for a few paces, and then resumes his normal gait when the kneecap slips back into position. It is usually spotted in puppies when they are between five and ten months of age. Sometimes both legs are affected, and if the dog is also overweight, the effect can be crippling.

Surgery may be needed in severe cases, but generally a Bichon will live with this condition and be largely unaffected, although arthritis may occur in the stifle in later life.

Summing up

It may give the Bichon owner cause for concern to find out about health problems that may affect their dog. But it is important to bear in mind that acquiring some basic knowledge is an asset, as it will allow you to spot signs of trouble at an early stage. Early diagnosis is very often the means to the most effective treatment.

Fortunately, the Bichon is generally a healthy and disease-free dog with his only visits to the vet being annual check-ups. In most cases, owners can look forward to enjoying many happy years with this affectionate and highly entertaining companion.

Useful addresses

Breed & Kennel Clubs

Please contact your Kennel Club to obtain contact information about breed clubs in your area.

UK

The Kennel Club (UK)
1 Clarges Street London, W1J 8AB
Telephone: 0870 606 6750
Fax: 0207 518 1058
Web: www.thekennelclub.org.uk

USA

American Kennel Club (AKC)
5580 Centerview Drive, Raleigh, NC 27606.
Telephone: 919 233 9767
Fax: 919 233 3627
Email: info@akc.org
Web: www.akc.org

United Kennel Club (UKC)
100 E Kilgore Rd, Kalamazoo,
MI 49002-5584, USA.
Tel: 269 343 9020
Fax: 269 343 7037
Web:www.ukcdogs.com/

Australia

Australian National Kennel Council (ANKC)
The Australian National Kennel Council is the administrative body for pure breed canine affairs in Australia. It does not, however, deal directly with dog exhibitors, breeders or judges. For information pertaining to breeders, clubs or shows, please contact the relevant State or Territory Body.

International

Fédération Cynologique Internationalé (FCI)
Place Albert 1er, 13, B-6530 Thuin, Belgium.
Tel: +32 71 59.12.38
Fax: +32 71 59.22.29
Web: www.fci.be/

Training and behavior

UK

Association of Pet Dog Trainers
Telephone: 01285 810811
Web: http://www.apdt.co.uk

Canine Behaviour
Association of Pet Behaviour Counsellors
Telephone: 01386 751151
Web: http://www.apbc.org.uk/

USA

Association of Pet Dog Trainers
Tel: 1 800 738 3647
Web: www.apdt.com/

American College of Veterinary Behaviorists
Web: http://dacvb.org/

American Veterinary Society of Animal Behavior
Web: www.avsabonline.org/

Australia

APDT Australia Inc
Web: www.apdt.com.au

For details of regional behaviorists, contact the relevant State or Territory Controlling Body.

Activities

UK

Agility Club
http://www.agilityclub.co.uk/

British Flyball Association
Telephone: 01628 829623
Web: http://www.flyball.org.uk/

USA

North American Dog Agility Council
Web: www.nadac.com/

North American Flyball Association, Inc.
Tel/Fax: 800 318 6312
Web: www.flyball.org/

Australia

Agility Dog Association of Australia
Tel: 0423 138 914
Web: www.adaa.com.au/

NADAC Australia
Web: www.nadacaustralia.com/

Australian Flyball Association
Tel: 0407 337 939
Web: www.flyball.org.au/

International

World Canine Freestyle Organisation
Tel: (718) 332-8336
Web: www.worldcaninefreestyle.org

Health

UK

British Small Animal Veterinary Association
Tel: 01452 726700
Web: http://www.bsava.com/

Royal College of Veterinary Surgeons
Tel: 0207 222 2001
Web: www.rcvs.org.uk

www.dogbooksonline.co.uk/healthcare/

Alternative Veterinary Medicine Centre
Tel: 01367 710324
Web: www.alternativevet.org/

USA

American Veterinary Medical Association
Tel: 800 248 2862
Web: www.avma.org

American College of Veterinary Surgeons
Tel: 301 916 0200
Toll Free: 877 217 2287
Web: www.acvs.org/

Canine Eye Registration Foundation
The Veterinary Medical DataBases
1717 Philo Rd, PO Box 3007,
Urbana, IL 61803-3007
Tel: 217-693-4800
Fax: 217-693-4801
Web: http://www.vmdb.org/cerf.html

Orthopedic Foundation of Animals
2300 E Nifong Boulevard
Columbia, Missouri, 65201-3806
Tel: 573 442-0418
Fax: 573 875-5073
Web: http://www.offa.org/

American Holistic Veterinary Medical
Association
Tel: 410 569 0795
Web: www.ahvma.org/

Australia

Australian Small Animal Veterinary
Association
Tel: 02 9431 5090
Web: www.asava.com.au

Australian Veterinary Association
Tel: 02 9431 5000
Web: www.ava.com.au

Australian College Veterinary Scientists
Tel: 07 3423 2016
Web: http://acvsc.org.au

Australian Holistic Vets
Web: www.ahv.com.au/